THE POWER OF
BEING CREATIVE

Featuring the story of Thomas Edison

Author
Patricia Metten

Art Illustrator
Stephen P. Krause

Editor, Layout and Research
Beatrice W. Friel

THE POWER OF
BEING CREATIVE

Featuring the story of Thomas Edison

Advisors
Paul and Millie Cheesman
Mark Ray Davis
Rodney L. Mann, Jr.
Roxanne Shallenberger
Dale T. Tingey

Publisher
Steven R. Shallenberger

AN EAGLE SYSTEMS
INTERNATIONAL
PUBLICATION
ANTIOCH, CALIFORNIA

Director and Correlator
Lael J. Woodbury

The Power of Being Creative
Copyright © 1981 by
Power Tales
Eagle Systems International
P.O. Box 1229
Antioch, California 94509

ISBN: 0-911712-89-5

Library of Congress Catalog No.: 81-50863

First Edition

Lithographed in USA by
COMMUNITY PRESS, INC.

A member of
The American Bookseller's Association
New York, New York

Dedicated to all creative people in the hope that they may
be inspired to develop their talents to benefit mankind.

THOMAS ALVA EDISON

Thomas Alva Edison, the seventh and last child of Samuel and Nancy Elliott Edison, was born on 11 February 1847 in Milan, Ohio. As a child he was quiet, thoughtful, and very inquisitive. Because he was not very sturdy, he was not sent to school until he was seven. His first teacher considered him incapable of learning, so his mother, who had been a teacher, took him out of school and taught him herself. Thus "one of the best informed men in the world on scientific subjects" had only three months of formal education.

Thomas' mother taught him how to think, and he became an avid reader. It was from the encyclopedia that Thomas first learned about chemistry and how to do experiments. His great passion for conducting experiments not only gained him much wide scientific knowledge, it also involved him in many legendary scrapes.

His first laboratory was set up in the cellar of his home in Port Huron, Michigan, where he had moved with his family in 1854.

When he was twelve years old he became a newsboy on the train which ran from Port Huron to Detroit. He was given a corner in the baggage car to keep his supply of newspapers, magazines, and candy. The railway company also allowed him to set up a laboratory there. During the six and a half hour layover in Detroit, Thomas would work in his laboratory or study chemistry and physics at the Detroit library. He also printed a paper on a secondhand press he had set up in the baggage car. He did very well as newsboy until one day when a bottle of phosphorus jarred off one of the shelves, broke on the floor, and started a fire. In his concern for the danger to his train, the angry conductor boxed Thomas' ears and put him off the train. As a result of this boxing Thomas gradually lost his hearing and became almost totally deaf in later years.

While working as a newsboy in the railroad station at Mt. Clemens, Michigan, Thomas saved the stationmaster's son by removing him from the path of a moving train. The grateful father taught Thomas telegraphy.

Thomas worked in telegraphy on and off for the next few years. One day he fixed the ticker tape system for a New York firm, and the grateful manager offered him a lucrative position. He worked for the firm until he was twenty-three, by which time he had saved enough money to open his own workshop. Between the years of 1870 and 1876 he patented 122 inventions.

In 1871 he married Mary G. Silwell, and it was said they were very happy. They had three children.

Giving up his efforts to simultaneously invent and manufacture, Thomas established a laboratory at Menlo Park in 1876. He hired skilled assistants to help him develop his ideas. About this time he started work on the first phonograph, and he created his carbon telephone transmitter, which helped to make the telephone commercially possible. In 1879 his practical incandescent lamp became a reality. Soon he became known as "The Wizard of Menlo Park."

In 1884 his wife, Mary, died of typhoid. Heartbroken, he buried himself deeper in his work and opened a big plant in Schenectady. In 1885 he hit upon the idea of moving pictures and began work on the forerunners of today's motion picture camera and projector.

When he was thirty-nine he met Mina Miller and they were married in 1886. They built a home in West Orange, New Jersey, and he moved his laboratory there from Menlo Park. They also had three children.

During World War I, Thomas became president of the United States Naval Consulting Board. This board was formed to develop inventions that would improve the defensive power of the Navy. During this time he was credited with 39 inventions of military importance. Some of these included a listening-device for detecting submarines, an underwater searchlight, a water-penetrating projectile, a device for detecting enemy airplanes, and a telephone system for ships.

During his lifetime Thomas patented 1,300 inventions. He worked in his laboratory at West Orange until a few weeks before his death at the age of eighty-four on 18 October 1931.

I must say, I do like people who read books, and so I know I'm going to like you.

I'm Leo, the light, right here on your page!

Do you think it would be a miracle, if light bulbs could talk?

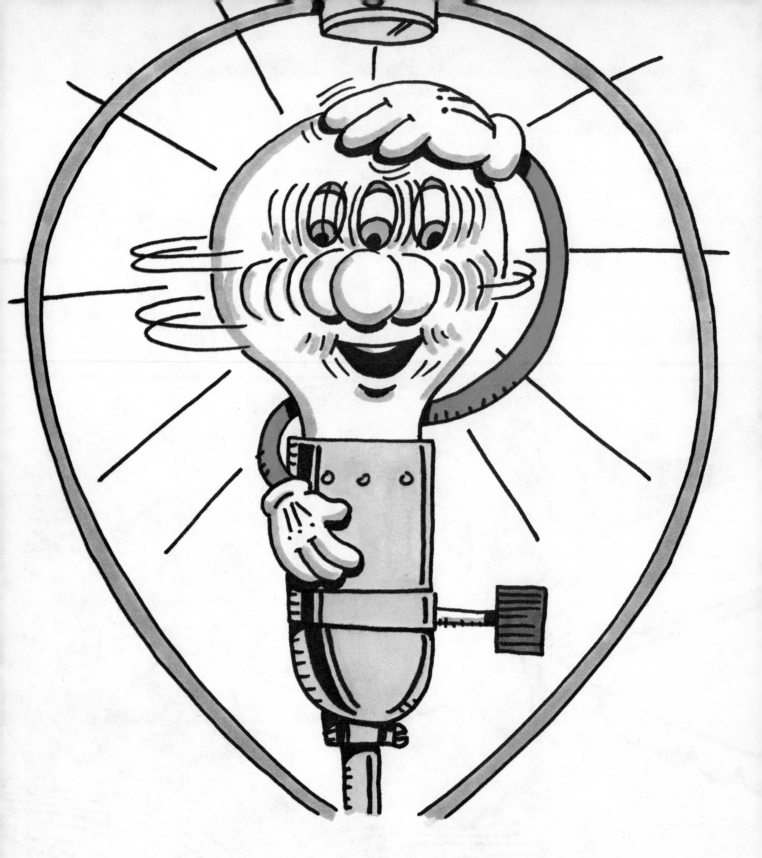

You're right. But since anything can happen in stories, I'm going to be talking a lot in this one. Let's go back to that word *miracle*. It *would* be a miracle for the light bulb in your lamp to talk. But it *is* a miracle for it to *light*! It was a very famous man, Thomas Edison, whose work made it possible for you to have electric light. He was one of the great creative talents of the world.

"Just a minute," you say. "What kind of talent?"

CREATIVE. Thomas Edison was a CREATIVE man. And he would want you to be curious enough to find out for yourself what the word CREATIVE means. I hope it will become clear as we go along. Thomas Edison's life was full of excitement and adventure, and I don't want you to miss any of it.

Tom was born in 1847 in Ohio. From the time he was very small, he wanted to know about everything. "Mother," he would say, "how does a hen hatch chickens?" Or he would ask his father, "What makes birds fly?" Perhaps he would ask one of his six brothers and sisters, "How does water put out a fire?"

"For heaven's sake," Tom's brothers and sisters would complain. "Why does Tom ask so many questions, Mother?"

Tom's mother was very patient. She had been a schoolteacher, and she tried to help Tom whenever she could. But some of his questions were too hard even for her to answer.

One day Tom said to himself, "If no one can tell me how a hen hatches chickens, I guess I'll have to find out for myself. I'll try an experiment. I can see that a hen hatches chicks out of eggs by sitting on them. So the thing for me to do is get some eggs and sit on them!"

Can you guess what happened to the eggs when Tom sat on them? You are right! I think the family was glad that he never did an experiment to see how water puts out a fire!

Tom's early experiment didn't work out too well, but he had started a way of thinking with his creative mind that was to stay with him all his life. This way of thinking led him to find out how things could be accomplished by trying something over and over again until he could work out the correct answer. Whenever he got an interesting idea he would keep working on it until his creative mind had made something out of it.

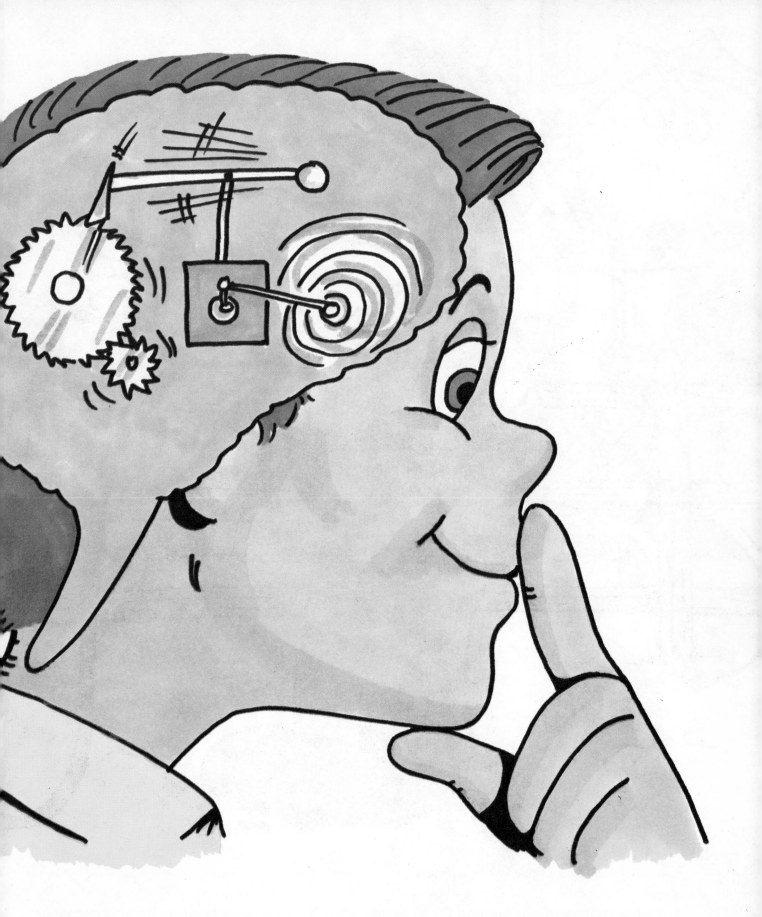

There was a clue just then as to what creative means. Did you get it? Now, in our story, Tom's mind was working, busy as ever.

"People fill balloons with a certain kind of gas," Tom thought, "and the balloons fly. If I could fill up one of my friends with gas, he might be able to fly too. What a great idea! I'll try it!" So Tom got some powder from

home and stirred it in a glass. When it was fizzing loudly, he gave it to a friend of his to drink. Unfortunately, Tom used too much powder. His friend became sick and dizzy and never left the ground.

"You can't make people fly the same way you make balloons fly," Tom said. "Now I know another thing that doesn't work. But I still have many more ideas to try."

Tom and his family moved to Michigan and he entered public school for the first time. Tom continued to ask questions until the schoolmaster became very angry. One day after Tom had been in school about three months, the district school inspector and the schoolmaster were talking.

"I've lost all patience with that Edison boy," said the schoolmaster. "What can you do with a child that's addled" (that means not right in the head).

Tom overheard their conversation. He was very hurt, for he hadn't thought there was anything wrong in asking questions. When he got home, he told his mother, and she hurried back to school.

"Sir," she said to the schoolmaster, "my son is not stupid. What's more, you ought to be ashamed of yourself for embarrassing a young boy." So his

mother, who had been a school teacher, took him out of school and taught him herself.

When Tom's mother began to teach him, she said, "Tom, we're going to go exploring!"

"That sounds wonderful, Mother. I like exploring.

"We'll make our study a game. Learning should be fun. There is so much of interest in the world, there will never be a minute for things to be dull."

With that kind of teaching, Tom learned very fast. When he was nine years old, he began creating experiments with chemicals. To begin with, he learned how to do experiments by reading in a chemistry book his mother had bought him. Often the rest of the family was curious about the more than 100 bottles of chemicals he had collected.

"Mother," he said one day, "some of my test tubes have been broken, and there's powder spilled from some of the bottles. I wish there was a way to keep the family from getting into my things."

"I'm sure you can think of a way," his mother said, smiling.

She was right. He did. Tom put labels that said "POISON" in big, black letters on all his bottles!

THINK ABOUT IT

1. Why didn't the eggs hatch when Tom sat on them?
2. How did it make you feel when the teacher said Tom was not right in the head?

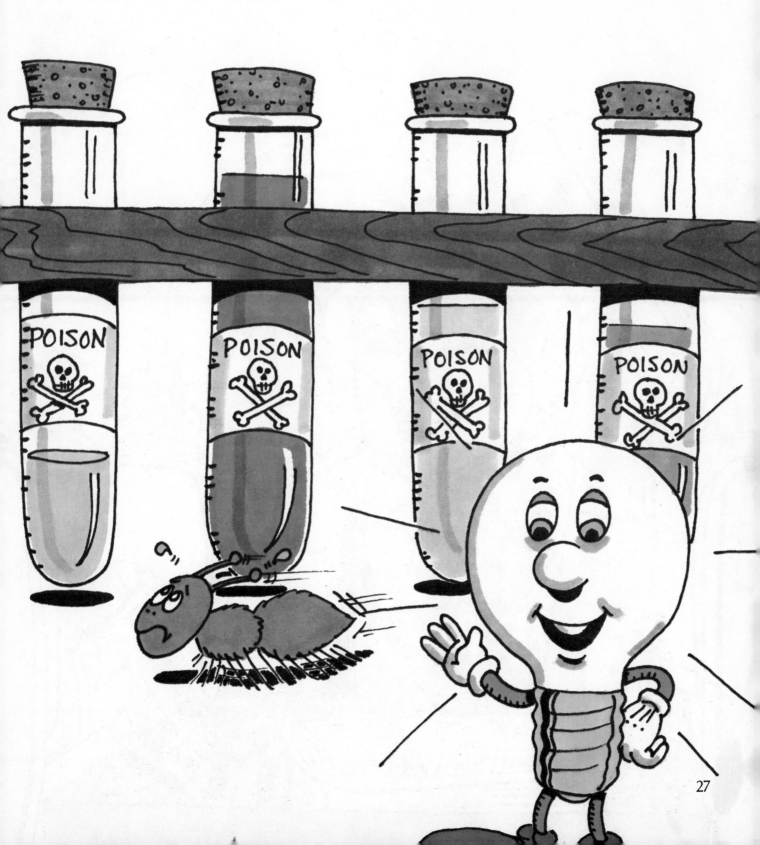

ON HIS OWN

"Paper! Candy! Peanuts! Paper!"

Three years had passed. Tom was now a big boy of twelve and sold papers and food on a train. However, he had something set up in the baggage car, where he could go in his spare time. Can you guess what it was?

"Where's that young man with the sandwiches?" asked a passenger. "I can never find him when I need him."

"I'll see if I can locate him for you, sir," replied the conductor. "You see, I've let the boy keep a few of his personal things in the baggage car for him to use in his spare time. It just looks like a bunch of harmless junk to me, but he generally does a good job for the passengers. He's even printed a newspaper with his own press back there in the baggage car. He's usually on hand when he's supposed to be. I'll have to go see what's wrong."

S–P–L–I–N–T–E–R!

"Great heavens! Is the train wrecked?" hollered the passenger.

"No, sir, I think I know what's happened and I'll take care of it, I assure you," called the conductor over his shoulder. He was hurrying down the aisle in the direction of the baggage car.

"Oh, hello, Mr. Hales," said Tom dazedly. He was sitting in the midst of shattered bottles, tumbled luggage, flames, and smoke. "I think something went wrong."

33

"I know a way to fix everything," yelled the conductor as he gathered up the printing press, chemicals, and Tom. "Just get off my train and stay off."

With that he slapped Tom hard on the ears and threw him and his possessions off the train.

Tom soon went back to selling newspapers, but this time in the railroad stations. One day a railroad car got loose and started to move toward the station agent's son, who was playing on the tracks. Tom saw this just in time and was able to save the boy. The station agent was so grateful, he asked Tom what he could do to repay him.

"Well, sir," said Tom. "I was wondering about the telegraph key in your office; the one you send messages with and it makes that tapping sound."

"Would you like to learn how to work a telegraph key and learn the code we use to tap out a message?"

"Yes, sir, I would like that very much," nodded Tom.

Before long, at the age of sixteen, Tom was working as a telegraph operator in Canada. Part of his job was to send a certain message exactly every hour.

"Sending the same message every hour is really a waste of time," he thought. "There must be a better way. Let me see. The hands of the clock are moving through the hours all the time. If there was just some way I could wire up a gadget to attach to. . . ." Tom's creative mind continued trying to solve the problem.

"Hooray! I've got it! I've invented a way to send the signal, even if I'm asleep," cried Tom. And he had. It worked so well, he almost lost his job when his boss found him asleep.

This was the first of Edison's inventions, all of which were created to make life better and more pleasant for everyone. Edison was always looking for "a better way."

By now I know you have found two words that I have used to help tell what CREATIVE means. They are "MAKE" and "INVENT." Please remember them as we finish Tom Edison's story. For the next 60 years Tom MADE and INVENTED one thing right after another. He became known as the greatest INVENTOR in history and changed the lives of people all over the world with his 1,100 inventions. Along with using his creative mind, he worked hard. He said his method was to "try everything" when he was inventing something.

One time, after he had tried 10,000 ideas, a friend told him it was too bad he had failed again.

"I have 10,000 ideas that won't work," said Edison, "but I have not failed."

THINK ABOUT IT

1. How did Tom go about developing an idea?
2. Why did Tom almost lose his job as a telegraph operator?

EXPERIENCE LEADS TO SUCCESS

Working in Boston at the age of 21, Edison traveled to Washington, D.C. He wanted to sell Congress his latest invention, a voting machine (a machine that counts votes). No one was interested in buying it, but this taught young Edison an important lesson—as unhappy experiences often do. He said, "I will never again invent something that nobody wants." From that time up until the end of his life he created inventions that would make life easier and better for people.

Edison now moved from Boston to New York, but he was so poor he had to sleep in the office of a friend.

In the office was a telegraph machine with a ticker tape. It recorded the changing price of gold for people who wanted to buy it. Edison spent a lot of time studying the machine. When it broke down, he was able to fix it after many others could not. The manager was so happy he offered Edison a job at a larger salary than he had ever earned. Tom continued getting more ideas on how to improve the machine, until one day the president of the company sent for him.

"Edison," the president said, "I'll come straight to the point. How much do you want for your ideas on improving my ticker tape?"

Young Edison had always been very poor, and he didn't know how much to ask for. He thought to himself, "Would it be right to ask for $5,000? I would gladly accept $3,000. Would $4,000 be better?" In desperation he blurted out, "Well, sir, suppose you make me an offer."

After thinking for a moment, the president said, "What would you say to $40,000?"

The room seemed to swim in front of Edison's eyes. He actually thought he was going to faint. He managed to reply slowly and softly, "Yes, I think that will be fair."

All the careful work that Edison had put into his creative ideas now began to show results. With the money he had just made he was able to open his first workshop in New Jersey. There, and in his next most famous laboratory in Menlo Park, he began to manufacture his improved ticker tape. He also helped to make the telephone a practical instrument.

Edison met and married Mary Silwell when he was 24. They had two boys and a girl. After thirteen years of marriage, Mary died. Since their children were still young and needed a mother, he married Mina Miller two years later. She was the daughter of a rich inventor, so she understood the kind of person Edison was. Three children were born to them—again two boys and a girl.

It was a good thing that Edison's new wife understood him. When his mind was creating an idea and he was planning it out in his head, he would forget about everything and everybody. He had had two serious ear injuries when only a boy. One had been from the conductor who had slapped his ears.

Later on his ears had been injured again. After these injuries he began to lose his hearing. As he grew older and became more deaf, he said he really didn't mind. It actually helped him concentrate on his work without being bothered by outside noises.

By now people were saying Edison was a genius. Although they felt he was gifted with many talents, they really didn't understand how hard he actually had to work at trying to create new ideas and getting them to work. So that there would be no misunderstanding about his work, Edison told people what his idea of "genius" was.

He said, "Genius is one percent inspiration and ninety-nine percent perspiration." He really proved this in the next two inventions, perhaps his most famous ones.

One day Edison said to himself, "There must be a way to record telegraph messages automatically. I have this disc which must revolve on this plate. Hmmmmm, but how can I get this disc to respond to sound vibrations?" On and on he worked, thinking it out in his head. Finally he believed he had something. Handing a sketch to his assistant, Edison said, "John, make this."

"What is it supposed to be?" asked John.

"Just make it and then we'll find out," replied Edison.

"I've never made anything like this before," said John, scratching his head.

"I know," Edison agreed. "There's never been anything like it before. I believe this will be something totally new."

John was always excited by Edison's new ideas. "Mr. Edison," he said, "I'm on my way!"

Sometime later he returned and handed Edison what he had made.

"Now can I know what it is?" he asked.

"Well," said Edison, trying to keep the excitement out of his voice, "I plan to see if this machine will talk."

John just stood there with his mouth open. He was not usually surprised at anything Edison did, but this was something no one had ever created.

Edison said a few words into the mouthpiece. No one breathed for a moment. Then the machine repeated Edison's words. Both men were so surprised they had to sit down. At last John exclaimed, "A talking machine, Mr. Edison!"

"Yes, John, I do believe that's exactly what we've got!" Edison had created the basic idea for his most original invention, the phonograph.

Now we come to my story. The INVENTION of me! Edison had worked for years and had tried to use thousands of substances for the wire inside his light bulb. Nothing would stay lit for very long. Edison worked on, not in the least discouraged.

"I know thousands of things that do not work. That is progress," he said. "I do know that my wire cannot be in air. Now, what substance can I use that will not deteriorate even in the absence of air?" On and on he worked. Then one night he placed a piece of burned sewing thread, that looked like thin wire, in a glass bulb. Electric current passed into the thread and it glowed brightly.

"Now," he said, "the real test. How long will it burn?" The next morning it was still burning! All that day and into the next day it burned! Only when Edison made some experiments on the light bulb did the light go out. But it had worked! He had created the electric light bulb, something the world needed very much.

Everyone was astounded by Edison's invention of the electric light bulb. He became known as "The Wizard of Menlo Park."

Moving to a larger laboratory, Edison worked on the development of motion pictures. He designed the first electric power station, worked at improving the storage battery, designed a cement mixer, and invented a duplicating machine. He lived to be eighty-four years old, his creative mind never ceasing to make and invent things to make life easier for everyone. He became one of the most honored men of his time.

Well, my friend, I'm very proud to be a part of the story of a man like Thomas Edison. If he were alive today, I think he would say, "Oh there are so many wonderful things just waiting to be invented. Get to work!"

Just think, you might even create a way to make *me* better!

I'd like that.

And so would Thomas Edison.